A DORLING KINDERSLEY BOOK

Senior Editor Jane Yorke
Editor Dawn Sirett
Senior Art Editor Mark Richards
Art Editor Jane Coney
Designer Margo Beamish-White
Production Marguerite Fenn

Photography by Michael Dunning
Additional Photography by Dave King
(pages 10–11)
Illustrations by Martine Blaney,
Dave Hopkins, and Colin Woolf
Animals supplied by Intellectual Animals
and Petsville

Eye Openers ®

First published in Great Britain in 1991
by Dorling Kindersley Limited,
9 Henrietta Street, London WC2E 8PS
Reprinted 1991, 1993

Copyright © 1991
Dorling Kindersley Limited, London

A CIP catalogue record for this book is
available from the British Library.

ISBN 0-86318-459-6

Reproduced by Colourscan, Singapore
Printed and bound in Italy by L.E.G.O., Vicenza

·EYE·OPENERS·

Pets

DORLING KINDERSLEY
London • New York • Stuttgart

Dog

puppy

Dogs need to be taken for walks outdoors. They like to chase after balls and sticks. A young dog is called a puppy. All dogs bark and wag their tails when they're excited.

 6

paw

ear

woof

tail

7

Budgie

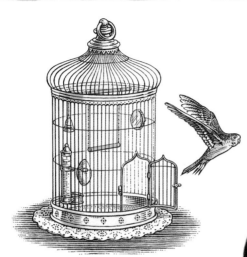

A budgie is a colourful bird that chirps. It lives in a cage. Budgies use their sharp beaks to crack open seeds.

tail

beak   feathers   claws

9

Cat

Cats have soft fur and like to be stroked. They purr when they are happy. A young cat is called a kitten. Kittens love to play and pounce. All cats sleep a lot during the day. They hunt mice at night.

miaow

claws

tail

11

Guinea pig

Guinea pigs are greedy about food. They grow fat if they do not get enough exercise. Guinea pigs can be very shy. They like to hide away from people in a nest of warm hay.

nose

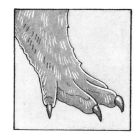

paw   ear

Rabbit

Rabbits hear very well with their big ears. They can run fast to escape from danger. Pet rabbits live in hutches. They like to eat carrots and fresh greens. Rabbits use their paws to dig holes in the ground.

paw

tail

ear

nose

Goldfish

Goldfish live in fish tanks. Their bodies are covered in bright, shiny scales. A goldfish uses its fins and tail to swim through the water. Goldfish must be fed special fish food every day.

gills

fin

tail

scales

17

Hamster

ear

Hamsters have large pouches in their cheeks that they use to collect seeds. They also gather food and store it in their cages to eat when they get hungry. Hamsters have sharp front teeth for gnawing their food.

teeth

 19

Tortoise

A tortoise carries a shell on its back. The shell is the tortoise's home and keeps the tortoise safe. When a tortoise is frightened, it pulls its head and feet into the shell. Tortoises move very slowly. They eat plants and insects.

head

tail

shell